✦ The Tale of the ✦
Great Bunny

The Story of the Magical Underground World of Chocolate

Based on a story by
Krystyna Lagowski

Adapted to verse by
David Mayerovitch

Illustrated by
Ron Berg

Created by
Capital C

Published by
Alphabet Editions
Toronto, Canada

1

Canadian Cataloguing in Publication Data

Mayerovitch, David
The tale of the Great Bunny: the story of the magical underground
world of chocolate

ISBN 1-896391-11-7

1.Easter eggs - Juvenile poetry. 2. Chocolate - Juvenile poetry. I. Berg, Ron.
II. Lagowski, Krystyna. III. Title

PS8576.A867T34 1998   jC811'.54   C97-932365-7
PZ8.3.M39Ta 1998

Story by: Krystyna Lagowski
Adapted by: David Mayerovitch
Illustrations: Ron Berg
Project Management: Capital C
Publishing Consultant: Alphabet Editions, an imprint of Alpha Corporation

Printed and Bound in Canada

I can barely remember the year I first started bringing chocolate treats to children like you on Easter morning. It was so very long ago. And ever since, children have been asking: Where does the chocolate come from? Why does it arrive? And why does everybody hunt for eggs on Easter morning?

Now I'm happy to be able to tell my story, complete with the first ever pictures of the magic land at the centre of the earth where my chocolate is made.

I hope that you keep this book for next year, and all of the Easter mornings that follow. That way, you can make the reading of this delightful tale an Easter tradition that your entire family can enjoy for years to come.

 - Great Bunny

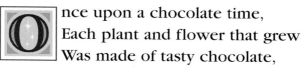

Once upon a chocolate time,
Each plant and flower that grew
Was made of tasty chocolate,
And all the trees were, too!

The children ran from tree to tree
To gobble chocolate bark,
And dined on dandelions made
Of chocolate rich and dark.

Sometimes the lucky children
Would be quick enough to spy
The furry, white Great Bunny
As he went hopping by.

His bunny nose would quiver
And his bunny eyes would shine,
As he nibbled tasty chocolate leaves
From every bush and vine.

But then one day it happened,
Filling hearts with doubt and fear,
The chocolate flowers, plants and trees
Began to disappear!

Great Bunny hopped around the world
And asked each child he met
To help him with a special plan,
"There's hope for chocolate yet!

"Go searching in the woods and fields,
And what you're searching for
Are chocolate seeds, so we can make
Our chocolate bloom once more.

"I'll plant them in a special place
That's way, way down below:
The very centre of the earth,
Where magic makes things grow!"

So kids brought lots of chocolate seeds
For Bunny's great collection,
And hens laid hollow chocolate eggs
To give the seeds protection.

And with each seed inside an egg
To keep it safe and sound,
Great Bunny set out on
His journey underground.

He crawled and crept down tunnels,
Turning left and twisting right,
And left behind a trail of chocolates,
Coloured bold and bright.

They'd help him find his way back out,
For knowing east from west
Is not the kind of thing
At which Great Bunny is the best.

He reached the centre of the earth,
And creatures living there
Helped him break the eggs,
And plant the seeds with loving care.

Then overnight there grew
Not only chocolate trees and flowers,
But chocolate houses, chocolate towns,
And candy-coated towers!

They called this wondrous chocolate world
The Land of Cadbury,
For "Cadbury" is the bunny word
For chocolate, don't you see.

Great Bunny found some eggs there
Of a most amazing kind:
The Purple Wishing Mini Eggs –
They're very hard to find!

They're hidden in a treasure chest,
Inside a secret cave,
Great Bunny is the only one
Who knows where they are saved.

Since kids like you once helped him
With this important thing,
The Bunny loves all children still,
And brings them treats each spring.

He asks his friends who live below
To help with his great plan,
Since they adore all children too,
They love to lend a hand.

The badgers mine the chocolate,
And then they melt it down,
The rabbits pour it into shapes,
While the mice just horse around.

The groundhogs are the engineers,
The beavers work . . . like beavers!
And all the while Great Bunny's there,
Inspiring each creature.

With each treat he leaves a paw print,
As a special sign
That the magic Land of Cadbury
Has made it taste so fine.

On Easter morning, every year,
Great Bunny makes his journey,
But no one ever sees him,
Because his visits are so early.

He slips into your house before
The dawn has grown too bright,
But he's scared he might get lost
Because he can't tell left from right.

So he leaves a trail of coloured chocolates
Lying on your floor,
In hopes that when he's finished
They will guide him to the door.

But sometimes, in his hurry,
He will leave some lying there.

That's your chance! Just follow them,
And they will show you where
You can find the chocolate treasure
That the Bunny loves to give.

He brought it 'cause it's Easter,
Just for you, 'cause you're a kid.

A chocolate statue you will find
Of Bunny, brave and bold,
And in his hand he's lifting up
A gift worth more than gold:

A Purple Wishing Mini Egg,
From the Land of Cadbury,
A chance for you to make a wish,
And dream of what might be!

Take that egg from Bunny's hand
And hold it to your heart,
Then shut your eyes and say this verse
To give your wish a start:

"O Purple Wishing Mini Egg,
While I am eating you,
I'm thinking of a special wish,
Please make my wish come true!"

Now eat the Purple Mini Egg,
Then look around your house,
There may be other treats
Great Bunny left about.

You might just find a Chocolate Egg
With chocolate seeds inside,
Have some fun while eating them,
But save one seed to hide.

An animal friend will find the seed
And take it down below,
And plant it there with loving care
So chocolate will always grow.

Now you know Great Bunny's tale
And all the friends he keeps,
And where his chocolate comes from,
And why he leaves you treats.

While down in the Land of Cadbury,
Which is chocolate through and through,
They're raising great big chocolate cheers
For wonderful kids like you!

Krystyna Lagowski *(Original story)*

Krystyna Lagowski has been writing since the age of six, and has managed to remain a child at heart. Currently, she is writing a collection of short stories about her childhood in Barry's Bay, Ontario.

David Mayerovitch *(Adaptation to verse)*

David Mayerovitch is a writer of wide experience in the entertainment and business worlds. His credits include "The Wayne & Shuster Comedy Special", the stage comedy *The Maltese Blue Jay* and updated lyrics for the Stratford Festival production of Gilbert and Sullivan's *The Gondoliers*. His other work ranges from journalism to speech writing and advertising copy for major Canadian corporations.

Ron Berg *(Illustration)*

Like most children, Ron Berg began drawing as soon as he could hold a crayon; unlike most of them, he never stopped. His whimsical illustration style has led to a long and successful career in the worlds of advertising and publishing. A father of two, Ron has illustrated several children's books including *The Owl and the Pussycat* (Scholastic), *Wynken, Blynken and Nod* (Scholastic) and *Night Fun* (Annick Press).